Published By Nicholas Thompson

@ Darren Chilson

Plant Based Diet: The Healthy About Weight Loss,

Weight Gain and Living a Healthy Life

All Right RESERVED

ISBN 978-87-94477-44-4

TABLE OF CONTENTS

Zucchini Frittata

Ingredients:

- 1 bell pepper (green, chopped)

- 4 zucchinis (cut in slices of 1-inch)

- 3 garlic cloves (peeled)

- 2 onion (diced)

- 7 mushrooms (chopped)

- 2 tbsp. of butter

- 5 eggs

- Pepper and salt (to taste)

- 2 cup of water

- 4 tbsps. of olive oil

- 1 tsp. of salt

- 2 and a 1 cup of mozzarella cheese (shredded)

- 4 tbsps. of parmesan cheese

Directions:

1. Start by preheating your oven at 160/175 degrees Celsius.
2. Take a large skillet and combine olive oil, water, green pepper, salt, garlic cloves, and zucchini. Simmer the mixture until the zucchini is soft—Cook for seven minutes.
3. Drain the water and remove the garlic; add mushroom, onion, and butter. Keep cooking until the onion turns transparent.
4. Add the eggs and keep stirring. Add pepper and salt for seasoning. Cook until the eggs are firm.
5. Add mozzarella cheese from the top.
6. Bake in the oven for ten minutes.

7. Remove the frittata from the oven and add parmesan cheese from the top. Place under the broiler for about 5 minutes.

8. Cut the frittata in wedges and serve warm.

Oatmeal And Strawberry Smoothie

Ingredients:

- Fourteen strawberries (frozen)

- 2 banana (cut in chunks)

- 3 tsps. of agave nectar

- 2 cup of almond milk

- 1 cup of rolled oats

- 1 tsp. of vanilla extract

Directions:

1. Add almond milk, strawberries, oats, agave nectar, banana, and vanilla extract in a food processor. Keep blending until smooth.

2. Serve with pieces of strawberry from the top.

Spicy Kale Chips

Ingredients:

- 1 teaspoon of cayenne pepper

- 1 teaspoon of chili powder

- 1 bunch of kale

- 2 tablespoons of olive oil

- Dash of salt

Directions:

1. Mix the salt, chili powder, and cayenne powder together, and set aside. Prepare the kale as the recipe above.

2. Use olive oil in coating the kale lightly. Sprinkle a mixture of pepper and salt. Bake for 8-10 minutes and serve.

3. There is the option to skip salt completely and simply use cayenne and/or the chili pepper options.

"Cheesy" Kale Chips

Ingredients:

- 2 tablespoons of olive oil

- 1 bunch of kale

- ½ teaspoons of sea salt

- 2 tablespoons of vegan parmesan "cheese"

Directions:

1. Prepare the kale like the previous recipes and coat with the olive oil.
2. Place the kale slices on the lined baking tray, and sprinkle salt, then coat with parmesan.
3. Bake for slightly longer, 10-11 minutes, until slightly brown or gold, then remove from the oven and serve.

Roasted Chickpeas

Ingredients:

- 1 teaspoon of salt

- 2 tablespoons of olive oil

- ½ of a can of chickpeas

- ½ teaspoon of chili powder (optional)

Directions:

1. Drain and rinse the chickpeas and dry, then pour into a bowl. Lightly coat all chickpeas in olive oil, then mix the chili powder and sea salt together, and coat the beans.
2. Transfer the chickpeas to a lined baking tray and bake for 20-25 minutes on 350 degrees.

Turmeric Steel Cut Oats

Ingredients:

- 1½ cup of water 2 cups for a thinner consistency

- 1 cup of non-dairy milk

- 1/3 teaspoon of turmeric

- ½ Teaspoon of cinnamon

- ¼ Teaspoon of cardamom

- ¼ Teaspoon of olive oil

- ½ Cup of steel cut oats use certified gluten-free if needed

- Salt to taste

- 2 tablespoons or more, of maple or other sweetener of your choice

Directions:

1. Toast oats in oil in a saucepan for a couple of minutes.
2. Add water and milk and bring it to a boil before letting it simmer.
3. Mix in the spices, salt, and maple and cook for about 8 minutes or until the oats are cooked to preference.
4. Taste and adjust sweet, and flavors as desired then let it cool to thicken. You can serve warm or chilled.
5. Garnish with strawberries, dried fruit or chia seeds.

Thai Noodles

Ingredients:

- 2 tablespoons of fresh lime juice (from 1 to 2 limes)

- 4 garlic cloves, minced

- 3 cups of frozen Asian-style vegetables

- 1 cup of mung bean sprouts

- 2 green onions, white and light green parts chopped

- 3 tablespoons of chopped, roasted, unsalted peanuts

- ¼ Cup of chopped fresh cilantro

- 8 ounces brown rice noodles or other whole-grain noodles

- 3 tablespoons of low-sodium soy sauce, or to taste

- 2 tablespoons of brown rice syrup or maple syrup

- 1 lime, cut into wedges

Directions:

1. Follow Directions: for cooking noodles.
2. Combine soy sauce, garlic, brown rice syrup, lime juice and cup water and bring to a boil. Stir in the veggies and cook for about 5 minutes or until crisp-tender.
3. Add the cooked noodles and mung bean sprouts and toss to coat then let it cook for a couple more minutes.
4. Garnish with cilantro, green onions, lime wedges and chopped peanuts.

Mediterranean Vegetable Spaghetti

Ingredients:

- ½ Jalapeño (optional)

- 2 tablespoons of dried herbs de Provence

- 2 tablespoons of tomato purée

- 2 tablespoons apple cider vinegar or juice of 1 lime

- 12 cherry tomatoes, quartered

- 1 zucchini, halved then sliced into thin 1-rounds

- 1 bunch spinach, chopped

- 10 ounces brown rice spaghetti

- 1 red bell pepper, cubed small

- 1 yellow bell pepper, cubed small

- 2 plum tomatoes, sliced into eighths (discard the seeds)

- Salt

- Handful of black olives

Directions:

1. Cook pasta, drain and set aside.
2. Sauté peppers, tomatoes, jalapeno, and herbs in a saucepan. Add water and let it simmer.
3. Add tomato puree and vinegar or lime juice and let it cook together for a few minutes until it becomes saucy.
4. Add cherry tomatoes, zucchini slices, and spinach. Mix well and cook for about 5 to 7 minutes.
5. Add olives and sauce to the pasts along with some herbs. Enjoy

Sweet Potato Slices With Fruits

Ingredients:

- 60 g organic peanut butter.

- 30ml pure maple syrup.

- 4 dried apricots, sliced.

- 1 sweet potato Topping.

- 30 g fresh raspberries.

Directions:

1. Peel and cut sweet potato into 1/2 cm thick slices.
2. Place the potato slices in a toaster on high for 5 minutes. Toast your sweet potatoes TWICE.
3. Arrange sweet potato slices onto a plate.
4. Spread the peanut butter over sweet potato slices.

5. Drizzle the maple syrup over the butter. Top each slice with an equal amount of sliced apricots and raspberries. Serve.

High-Protein Apple Pie Smoothie

Ingredients:

- 1 medium apple, peeled, cored and sliced.

- 1/2 frozen banana.

- 1/2 tsp vanilla extract.

- 1 tsp maple syrup.

- 1 tsp cinnamon.

- 1 cup of almond milk.

- 1 scoop plant-based vanilla protein powder.

- 1/4 cup gluten-free rolled oats.

- Pinch nutmeg.

- Pinch ground ginger.

- Ice, as needed.

Directions:

1. Add all active ingredients to a high speed mixer.
2. Mix on high till smooth.
3. Add ice into a mixer if you need a cold smoothie.
4. Pour into a glass and take pleasure in.

Pumpkin Sourdough Protein Pancakes

Ingredients:

Overnight sponge:

- 1/2 cup chickpea flour (or any other gluten-free flour).

- 1/2 cup almond milk.

- 1-2 tbsp maple syrup.

- 1/4 cup gluten-free sourdough starter.

- 1/4 cup pumpkin puree.

In the morning:

- 1/2 tsp turmeric.

- 1/4 cup raw cacao nibs (or non-diary chocolate chips).

- A handful of sliced pecans (optional however extremely advised!).

- 1/2 tsp baking soda.

- 1 flax egg (1 tbsp ground flaxseed + 3 tbsp water).

- 1 tsp pumpkin spice.

- 1 tsp cinnamon.

- 1 tsp baking powder.

Directions:

1. The night before making the pancakes, position the overnight sponge ingredients into a non-reactive bowl. Mix well, cover with plastic wrap and let it sit overnight.

2. In the morning, before you make the pancakes, add all the other ingredients (other than baking powder and baking soda) into the overnight sponge. Stir well.

3. Heat a non-stick pan over medium heat.

4. Add baking soda and baking powder to the batter and carefully stir them in.

5. Put 1/4 cup of the batter onto the pan for each pancake and fry until you see bubbles forming on the surface area of the pancakes and the edges dry out.

Cardamom & Walnut Quinoa Porridge

Ingredients:

- 250ml unsweetened almond milk

- 2 ripe peaches, cut into pieces

- 1 teaspoon walnut syrup

- 75g quinoa

- 25g porridge oats

- 4 cardamom pods

Directions:

1. Place The quinoa, ginger, and cardamom pods in a little saucepan with 250ml water along with 100ml of this almond milk. Bring to the boil, then simmer gently for 15 mins, stirring periodically.

2. Pour From the residual almond milk and cook
    for 5 mins longer until creamy.

3. Eliminate That the cardamom pods, spoon
    into jars or bowls, and shirt with all the berry
    and maple syrup.

Protein Pancakes

Ingredients:

For your batter

- 1 moderate banana, mashed

- 2 tablespoon walnut syrup

- Coconut oil, for frying

- 2 tbsp ground flaxseeds

- 20g floor peppers

- 300ml soya milk

- 200g quinoa flour

For Your Blueberry Chia Jam (Leaves 200ml)

- 1-2 tablespoon walnut syrup, to taste

- 2 tsp lemon juice

- 200g blueberries, mashed

- 2 tablespoon chia seeds

For your pile

- 2 tbsp hulled hemp seeds

- Mixed berries

- 100g coconut milk or Greek yogurt

- 1 tablespoon pistachio nuts or pumpkin seeds, sliced, toasted if you prefer

Directions:

1. In A small bowl, stir the flaxseeds using 6 tablespoons water and set aside to soak as you make the shake.

2. Mash the tomatoes using a fork at a pan then place above a low-medium heat until syrupy and bubbling.

3. Remove from the heat and stir in the chia seeds, maple syrup, and lemon juice. Leave to cool slightly then move to a little serving jar.

4. Place the ground almonds, milk, flour, banana, maple syrup, and a pinch of Salt in a blender. Stir the carrot to be certain it is now thick and gloopy, such as an egg, then tip in the mixture and blitz until thick and smooth.

5. Heating 1 teaspoon of coconut oil in a large skillet over a moderate heat and add tbsp dollops of batter to the pan.

6. Cook for a few mins on 2 side before the edges are browning, and bubbles have formed on top.

7. When the light, white batter has turned into a sandy color, flip over using a spatula, and cook for a few mins till dark golden brown.

8. Set aside and keep warm as you repeat the procedure with the remaining batter, adding a

different teaspoon of coconut oil with every
batch. You need to make about 16 pancakes.

9. Pile The sausage high between 2 plates,
    alternating the layers together with spoonfuls
    of jam and yogurt.

10. Dollop any leftover yogurt and a spoonful of
    jam in addition to scattering over the nuts,
    berries and seeds to function. The leftover
    jam will keep in the refrigerator for up to 1
    week.

Blackcurrant Compote

Ingredients:

- Juice 1/2 lemon

- 500g blackcurrants

- 100g golden caster sugar

Directions:

1. Place 2 tablespoons water and the lemon juice in a large saucepan, bring to the boil, then put in the blackcurrants and simmer till broken down.

2. Hint From the golden caster sugar and deliver about 105C on a temperature probe. Pour into sterilized jars and leave to cool. Will keep in the refrigerator for up to 3 months.

Green Probiotic Smoothie

Ingredients:

- 1 fist baby spinach

- 1 teaspoon grass fed collagen

- ¼ Cup frozen mixed berries

- Ha kombucha tea

- 1 teaspoon chia seeds

- ¼ Avocado, peeled and pitted

- ¼ Cup coconut milk

Directions:

1. In a food processor mix all the ingredients together with a discount for chia seeds. After the ingredients are blended until smooth. Then add in chia seeds, do some quick pulse to mix well.

Lime, Cucumber, And Celery Shake

Ingredients:

- Ice cup ice

- ¼ Cup of water

- 2 stalks and bite-sized portion of celery heart

- ½ Small cucumbers, sliced, peeled, sliced and deseeded.

- Ice lime juice

- 1 alcohol pill (optional)

Directions:

1. Put everything in a food processor and mix easily. Strain the smoothie to get the juice. Serve with 3 to 4 cubes of ice.

Sweet Potato And Onion Patties

Ingredients:

- 1 large or 2 small or medium eggs

- Sea salt / ground black pepper, as desired

- Paprika, ½ tsp

- Chili-pepper, ½ teaspoon

- 1 large or 2 med sweet potatoes

- 1 small onion, white or yellow, diced finely

- Olive oil for cooking

Directions:

1. To prepare the sweet potatoes, scrub, peel and slice them into halves, thirds, or sizes that are comfortable to shred through a grate.

2. Using a large grater, shred all the sweet potato and set aside.

3. Peel the onion and slice in 1 and shred or finely dice to mix with the sweet potato.

4. Mix these 3 ingredients well with a fork, then add in the eggs, whisking and blending evenly.

5. Add in the sea salt, black pepper, paprika, and chili pepper, to create the patty batter.

6. Over med heat and a lg skillet warm olive oil.

7. As the skillet is in the process of warming up, form 2-inch or 3-inch sized patties to fry on both sides of the skillet.

8. If desired, add a light sprinkle of sea salt and/or the spices and seasoning of your choice.

9. Cook on each side for about 2 minutes, or until the result is golden in color.

10. Serve immediately garnished with sliced parsley, coriander, and/or sour cream.

Sweet Potato Baked With Garlic And Kale

Ingredients:

- Kale (any variety, finely sliced with stems removed), 1 cup

- Sea salt

- 2 crushed garlic cloves

- Sweet potatoes (1 small or medium)

- Olive oil

Directions:

1. Peel, wash, and scrub the sweet potato and make a few slices into the top, or poke with a fork. Wrap the potatoes in tin foil and poke with the fork a couple of times.

2. Set oven to 350 degrees, once preheated, add the dish for approximately 45-60 min or until the sweet potatoes are tender and flaky inside.

3. They can be baked directly in the rack in the oven or a pan. As the sweet potatoes bake, prepare a skillet with 2 tablespoon of olive oil.

4. Toss in the crushed garlic cloves, sliced kale, and sea salt. Saute on medium until the kale is crispy (or almost crispy).

5. If the kale is d2 before the sweet potatoes, turn off the stovetop and cover with a lid until they are ready.

6. Serve the sweet potatoes with a drizzle of olive oil and top with the garlic and kale mix to serve.

Guacamole Lettuce Boats

Ingredients:

- 1 tablespoon of chopped onion

- 1 teaspoon of chopped cilantro

- 1 tablespoon of lemon juice

- 1/2 avocado

- A pinch of iodized sea salt

- 4 romaine lettuce leaves, washed and dried

Directions:

1. To make the guacamole just place all the ingredients in the blender and process them until it's smooth.

2. Then just add the guacamole over the lettuce.

Roasted Broccoli With Cauliflower "Rice" And Pan-Fried Onions

Ingredients:

For the Cauliflower "Rice"

- 1 tablespoon of lemon juice

- A pinch of sea salt

- 1/4 teaspoon of curry

- 1 a medium head of a riced cauliflower

- 1 tablespoon of avocado oil

For the Broccoli

- 1 1/2 cups of cut broccoli buds

- 1 tablespoon of avocado oil

- A pinch of sea salt

For the Sautéed onions

- 1/2 tablespoon avocado oil

- A pinch of salt

- Diced onions

Directions:

1. Preheat the oven to 325°F.

2. Sauté the cauliflower in a medium pan with 1 tablespoon of avocado oil, and the lemon juice, curry powder, and a pinch of salt until it is tender, about 3 to 5 minutes.

3. Pass it to a plate and keep it warm. Wipe the pan clean.

4. Put the broccoli in an oven safe plate with 1 tablespoon of the oil.

5. Roast it for 15 minutes, blending it twice, until it is tender.

6. Add a tad of salt.

7. Reheat the frying pan and when it is hot, add the remaining tablespoon avocado oil, the diced onion and a pinch of salt.

8. Fry until tender, stirring often, for about 5
    minutes.

9. To serve, place the cauliflower "rice" on a
    plate and on top of it, the broccoli and stir-
    fried onions.

Australian Breakfast Omelet

Ingredients:

- 1 small avocado, peeled, pitted and cubed into small pieces

- Salt and freshly ground black pepper to taste

- 4 large organic eggs

- 2 tablespoons olive oil, divided

- 1 teaspoon chives, fresh minced

- 2 small beets, peeled and spiralized with Blade C

Directions:

1. Using a large pan, heat 1 tablespoon olive oil over medium heat and cook the beet noodles for about 7 minutes.

2. Remove from heat and set aside.

3. Add to your mixing bowl, salt, pepper and
    eggs then beat well.
4. Heat the remaining oil in large frying pan over
    medium heat.
5. Add your egg mixture to your pan and spread
    the eggs over pan using a wooden spoon.
6. Cook the egg mixture for 12 minutes.
7. Place the beets and avocado over the eggs.
8. Carefully, fold the omelet over the beet
    noodles and avocado and cook for 2 minutes.
9. Cut the omelet into 3 portions and serve with
    the chives for garnish.

Avocado Cups

Ingredients:

- 2 ripe avocados, halved, pitted and scoop out about 2 tablespoons of flesh

- 1 tablespoon chives, fresh minced

- 4 organic eggs

- Salt and freshly ground black pepper to taste

Directions:

1. Preheat your oven to 425°Fahrenheit.
2. Arrange the avocado halves in a small baking dish, with the cut side facing upwards.
3. In a mixing bowl, break an egg then transfer it into an avocado 1.
4. Repeat this step with the remaining eggs.
5. Carefully, place into your oven and bake for 20 minutes or until you have reached the desired d2ness reached.

6. Serve immediately, sprinkle with salt and

    pepper and chives

Awesome Chipotle Bean Stew

Ingredients:

Veg

- 1 cup celery cut up into chunks

- 2 cups of bell peppers cut up into chunks

- 2 cups firm tomatoes cut up into chunks

- 1 large yellow onion diced

- 3 cups kale, bok choy or dark green cabbage to add in the final 30 minutes of cooking

- Unsalted cooked cashews, added once the stew is cooked

- 4 cups of waxy potatoes cut up into large chunks

- 1 1/s cups of dry pinto beans (or similar)

- 2 cups of carrots cut up into chunks

Broth

- 2 – 4 tablespoons arrowroot powder

- 4 garlic segments mashed

- 2 tablespoons chipotle chili spice

- 2 cups of water

- 6 cups vegetable broth, homemade or low sodium shop brought (this needs to be sufficient to cover all the vegetables when ingredients are placed into the slow cooker).

- 1 tablespoon garlic powder

- 1 tablespoon onion powder

- Freshly ground black pepper to taste

- Salt to taste

Directions:

1. Put the vegetable broth and water into a slow cooker (note that sodium will make the beans tough, so try to use low sodium broth).

2. Add the prepared veg except the greens and cashews. There should be about an inch of liquid covering the vegetables, add more broth if required.

3. Cook on high for 5 to 6 hours or on low at 8 to 9 hours.

4. In the final 1 hour of cooking put the arrowroot powder, garlic, chipotle, garlic powder and onion powder with a ¼ cup of water. Blend on high speed until smooth (add more liquid if required). Add this to the broth in the slow cooker and whisk it in until well combined.

5. Chop the greens (removing any coarse stalks) and add to the stew allow to wilt.

6. Finally, add the cashew nuts and stir well.

7.   Serve immediately.

Vegetable Mousekey

Ingredients:

- 4 tomatoes, skins removed (soak in boiling water for 5 minutes) and chopped

- 1 tablespoon of tomato puree

- 2 tablespoons apple cider vinegar

- 1 tablespoon mixed herbs

- 3 ounces of walnuts, chopped

- 1-ounce whole meal breadcrumbs

- Salt and pepper to taste

- 1-ounce whole meal flour

- ½ pint almond milk

- 5 tablespoons vegetable oil

- 1 large eggplant cut into thin slices

- 1 large onion chopped

- 4 ounces mushrooms sliced

- 2 garlic cloves crushed

- Extra walnuts to garnish

Directions:

1. Pre-heat the oven to 350 degrees Fahrenheit

2. In a skillet heat 2 tablespoons of oil and fry the eggplant on both sides, drain on kitchen paper and set aside.

3. Add another 1 tablespoon of oil to the pan and sauté the chopped onion until cooked through.

4. Add the mushrooms and garlic to the pan and cook for a further 5 minutes on a medium heat.

5. Add the tomatoes, tomato puree, vinegar and herbs and cook on a low heat until it forms a sauce.

6. Add the walnuts, breadcrumbs, salt and pepper, add a drop more oil if necessary.

7. In a saucepan, make the white sauce by adding any remaining oil, flour and almond milk, whisk continually for around 5 minutes over a very gentle heat until it has become smooth and thick.

8. Lightly grease a shallow ovenproof dish. Place some of the eggplant slices next to 2 another on the base.

9. Spoon 1 of the nut mixture into the dish and cover with 1 of the white sauce.

10. Place the remaining eggplant slices on top and add another layer of nut mixture and white sauce.

11. Bake in the oven for 30 minutes. 1way
    through cooking time you can add the extra
    nuts.

12. Serve with a side of salad or potatoes and
    vegetables as desired.

Classic Vegan Pancakes

Ingredients:

- ¼ teaspoon salt

- 1 cup plant-based milk (such as soy or almond milk) 1 tablespoon vegetable oil

- 1 teaspoon vanilla extract

- 1 cup all-purpose flour

- 2 tablespoons granulated sugar

- 2 teaspoons baking powder

Directions:

1. In a mixing bowl, whisk together the flour, sugar, baking powder, and salt.
2. In a separate bowl, combine the plant-based milk, vegetable oil, and vanilla extract.

3. Pour the wet ingredients into the dry
    ingredients and whisk until just combined. Be
    careful not to overmix; a few lumps are okay.

4. Heat a non -stick skillet or griddle over
    medium heat and lightly grease with oil or
    cooking spray.

5. Scoop about ¼ cup of batter onto the skillet
    for each pancake.

6. Cook until bubbles form on the surface, then
    flip and cook for another minute or until
    golden brown.

7. Repeat with the remaining batter.

8. Serve the pancakes warm with your favorite
    toppings, such as maple syrup, fresh berries,
    or vegan butter.

9. Enjoy these classic vegan pancakes as a
    comforting and delicious breakfast option.

Vegan Banana Bread

Ingredients:

- 1 teaspoon baking soda

- ½ teaspoon salt

- ½ teaspoon ground cinnamon

- 2 cups mashed ripe bananas (about 4 medium bananas) ⅓ cup melted coconut oil or vegetable oil ⅓ cup maple syrup or agave nectar

- ½ cup plant-based milk (such as almond or oat milk) 1 teaspoon vanilla extract

- 2 cups all-purpose flour

- Optional: ½ cup chopped nuts or chocolate chips

Directions:

1. Preheat the oven to 350°F (175°C) and lightly grease a 9x5-inch loaf pan.

2. In a large mixing bowl, combine the mashed bananas, melted coconut oil, maple syrup or agave nectar, plant -based milk, and vanilla extract.

3. In a separate bowl, whisk together the flour, baking soda, salt, and ground cinnamon.

4. Gradually add the dry ingredients to the wet ingredients, stirring until just combined. Avoid over mixing.

5. Fold in the optional chopped nuts or chocolate chips if desired.

6. Pour the batter into the prepared loaf pan and smooth the top with a spatula.

7. Bake for 50-60 minutes or until a toothpick inserted into the center comes out clean.

8. Allow the banana bread to cool in the pan for 10 minutes, then transfer it to a wi re rack to cool completely before slicing.

9. Enjoy a slice of this moist and flavorful vegan banana bread as a delightful snack or breakfast option.

Amy's Spinach Pizza with a Cauliflower Crust

Ingredients:

- 1/2 teaspoon ocean salt, ideally iodized

- 1/2 teaspoon split dark pepper

- 1/2 teaspoon dried oregano

- Extra-virgin olive oil for lubing the container

- 1 little head cauliflower, cut into little florets

- 1 fed or omega-3 egg, gently beaten

- 1/2 cup destroyed wild ox or goat mozzarella

Topplng

- Cleaved vegetables of your decision (discretionary)

- 1 cup ground Pecorino Romano cheddar

- Squeeze ocean salt, ideally iodized

Directions:

1. Flush the cauliflower. You will have around 3 cups. Move to a microwave-safe dish and microwave on high for 8 minutes, until cooked. Permit to cool, mixing infrequently. Spot a rack in the stove. Warmth the broiler to 450°F. Oil a 10-inch ovenproof skillet with olive oil.

2. Spot the cooled riced cauliflower in a dishtowel, and turn and crush to evacuate all the dampness. Move to a blending bowl. Include the egg, mozzarella, salt, pepper, and oregano. Blend well.

3. Press the blend equitably in the griddle over medium warmth on the stove top, fresh the cauliflower hull for a couple of moments.

4. Move to the stove and heat for 15 minutes, until brilliant. Let cool for 5 minutes, and include the garnish.

5. Disperse the mozzarella equitably over the pizza base and spread the spinach. Include any extra vegetables. Sprinkle with the Pecorino Romano cheddar and include a touch of salt. Prepare for an extra 10 minutes, until the cheddar has softened.

6. Veggie lover VERSION: Replace the egg with 1 VeganEgg and use Kite Hill Ricotta "cheddar" in lieu of the cheeses.

Flame broiled Portabella-Pesto Mini "Pizzas"

Ingredients:

Basil pesto

- 1/2 cup pine nuts or pecans

- 3 1-inch solid shapes Parmigiano Reggiano

- 1 cup pressed new basil leaves

- 1/4 cup extra-virgin olive oil

Small scale "PIZZAS"

- Ocean salt, ideally iodized, to taste

- Split dark pepper, to taste

- 1/2-inch-thick cuts

- 2 enormous portabella mushroom, stems
  expelled extra-virgin coconut or olive oil

- 2 cuts Italian prosciutto

- 1 ball wild ox mozzarella, cut into pieces

Directions:

1. Make the pesto. In a smaller than expected nourishment processor, beat the basil, olive oil, pine nuts, and cheddar until very much mixed.

2. Make the "pizzas." set 2 burner of a gas barbecue to high or spot a flame broil container on the stove with burner set to medium-high warmth with the fumes fan on. Rub the top side of the mushrooms with oil, place on the barbecue or flame broil dish, top side up, and flame broil for around 5 minutes, until the tops start to dark colored somewhat. Flip over and barbecue, gill side up, for an additional 5 minutes. Expel the mushrooms from the flame broil or burner. Leave the warmth on.

3. Spoon 3 tablespoons of pesto onto the gill side of 2 mushroom, include 1 cut prosciutto, masterminding it to fit perfectly in the gill cup, and afterward top with a large portion of the mozzarella cuts. Rehash with the other mushroom. If cooking on a flame broil, return the mushrooms to the barbecue, close the hood, and flame broil until the cheddar starts to dissolve, around 5 minutes.

4. If cooking inside, return the flame broil skillet to the stove top for around 5 minutes; on the other hand, spread the barbecue dish with a glass meal spread to "steam" for 5 minutes.

5. To serve. Season to taste with salt and pepper.

Coconut-Almond Flour Muffin In A Mug

Ingredients:

- ½ teaspoon aluminum-free baking powder

- Pinch sea salt, preferably iodized

- 1 packet stevia, or 2 teaspoons Just Like Sugar

- 1 tablespoon water

- 1 large pastured or omega-3 egg, lightly beaten

- 1 tablespoon extra-virgin coconut oil, melted

- 1 tablespoon extra-virgin olive oil or macadamia nut oil

- 1 tablespoon coconut flour

- 1 tablespoon almond flour

Directions:

1. Place the ingredients in an 8- to 12-ounce
    microwave-safe mug, mixing well with a fork
    or spatula. Be sure to scrape the bottom and
    sides. Let it sit for a few seconds.

2. Microwave on high for 1 minute plus 25 to 30
    seconds.

3. Using a pot holder, remove the mug from the
    microwave and invert, shaking out the muffin.
    Let cool for a couple of minutes before eating.

Cranberry-Orange Muffins

Ingredients:

- ¼ cup Just Like Sugar or xylitol

- 3 large pastured or omega-3 eggs

- 1 tablespoon orange zest

- ½ cup dried, unsweetened cranberries

- ¼ cup coconut flour

- ¼ teaspoon sea salt, preferably iodized

- ¼ teaspoon baking soda

- ¼ cup extra-virgin coconut oil, melted

Directions:

1. Heat the oven to 350°F. Line a standard 6-cup muffin tin with paper liners.

2. Place the coconut flour, salt, and baking soda in a food processor fitted with an S-blade.

3. Add the coconut oil, Just Like Sugar, eggs, and orange zest. Pulse until blended. Remove the processor blade and stir in the cranberries by hand.

4. Scoop the batter into the muffin tins, filling to just beneath the rim. Bake for 20 minutes. Let cool on a rack for 15 minutes before serving.

Buffalo Cauliflower

Ingredients:

- 2 large egg

- 7 cups of cauliflower florets

- 3 cups of garlic croutons

- 2-fourth cup of parmesan cheese (grated)

- 2 serving of cooking spray

- 1 cup of buffalo sauce

- 4 tbsps. of mayonnaise

For the dipping sauce:

- Blue cheese salad dressing

- 2 tsp. of black pepper (ground)

- 2-fourth cup of each

- Sour cream

Directions:

1. Start by preheating your oven to 230 degrees Celsius. Use a cooking spray for greasing a baking tray.

2. Combine mayonnaise, buffalo sauce, and egg in a bowl. Toss the florets of cauliflower in the mixture of sauce and coat properly.

3. Spread the tossed florets on the baking tray.

4. Add the croutons on a blender and pulse them into crumbs. Add the cheese and pulse again. Spread the mixture of cheese and croutons over the florets of cauliflower.

5. Bake for fifteen minutes until tender and browned. Allow the florets to sit for 5 minutes.

6. Mix all the ingredients for the dipping sauce.

7. Serve cauliflower florets with dip sauce by the side.

Garlic Bread And Veggie Delight

Ingredients:

- 2 tomato (chopped)

- 2 tsp. Of salt

- 3 tsps. Of each

- Basil (minced)

- Oregano (minced)

- 2 baguette

- Four tsps. Of garlic powder

- 2 cup of olive oil

- 2 garlic clove (chopped)

- 2 eggplant (cubed)

- 2 zucchini (cubed)

- 7 tsps. Of butter

Directions:

1. Take a large skillet and add olive oil to it. Add garlic and fry for 3 minutes until browned.

2. Add the zucchini and eggplant to the skillet and cook for 5 minutes. Make sure that the eggplant is tender and brown.

3. Add the chunks of tomato and combine the veggies; add basil, oregano, and salt. Cook for 3 minutes and remove from heat.

4. Preheat oven 140/165 degrees Celsius.

5. Slice the baguette into 2-inch slices, approximately twelve slices. Add butter and garlic powder on the bread slices and place them on the oven rack. Heat the bread for 5 minutes.

6. Arrange the heated bread slices on a plate. Top the slices with vegetables. Serve immediately.

Rice Pudding

Ingredients:

- 1 ½ cups of low carb sweetener (monk fruit or swerve is recommended)

- 1 teaspoon of vanilla extract

- 1 cup of water

- 2 tablespoons of coconut oil or butter

- 1 cup of basmati rice (uncooked)

- 4 cans of coconut milk (unsweetened) or 6 measured cups

- Cinnamon for the topping

Directions:

1. In a large cooking pot, combine the coconut milk, basmati rice, sweetener, and water, and

bring to a boil, then reduce heat and continue
to cook and simmer for about 2 hour.

2. Add in the vanilla extract and simmer, stirring
regularly until the mixture thickens.

3. Add in the coconut butter or oil and simmer a
few more minutes, then remove from heat to
cool. Serve sprinkled with cinnamon.

Chia Seed Pudding

Ingredients:

- 2 cup of coconut milk

- 2 teaspoons coconut cream or butter

- 1 teaspoon of vanilla extract

- 1 cup of chia seeds

- ¼ cup of sweetener (low carb sweetener or maple syrup)

Directions:

1. In a small container or bowl, whisk together all the above ingredients.
2. Chia seeds tend to stick to utensils, and it may take a few minutes to thoroughly blends everything. Store in the refrigerator for 3 hours or more, then remove to serve.

3. The pudding should have a thick, custard-like consistency that is easy to scoop and serve.

4. This recipe serves 2-3 and takes only a few minutes to prepare, before chilling in the refrigerator.

Mexican Lentil Soup

Ingredients:

- 1 tablespoon cumin

- ¼ Teaspoon smoked paprika

- 1 teaspoon oregano

- 2 cups diced tomatoes and the juices

- 4 ounces diced green chilies

- 2 cups green lentils, rinsed and picked over

- 8 cups vegetable broth

- ½ Teaspoon salt

- A dash (or more) of hot sauce, plus more for serving

- Fresh cilantro, for garnish

- 2 tablespoons extra virgin olive oil

- 1 yellow onion, diced

- 2 carrots, peeled and diced

- 2 celery stalks, diced

- 1 red bell pepper, diced

- 3 cloves garlic, minced

- 1 avocado, peeled, pitted, and diced, or garnish

Directions:

1. Sauté onions, celery, bell pepper and carrots in a pan for about 5 minutes then add garlic, cumin, paprika, and oregano and let it cook for another minute.

2. Add in tomatoes, chilies, lentils, broth, and salt to taste and bring to a simmer until lentils are tender.

3. Season with salt and pepper as necessary

4. Serve it garnished with fresh cilantro,
    avocado, and a few dashes of hot sauce.

Walnut Meat Tacos

Ingredients:

Walnut tacos:

- ½ Teaspoon of chili powder

- A tablespoon of tamari

- 6 Taco shells (organic & gluten-free)

- 1½ cups de-shelled walnuts

- 1 teaspoon of garlic powder

- ½ Teaspoon of cumin

Toppings:

- Lime cashew sour cream:

- 1 Cup cashews soaked overnight (or soaked at least 10 mins in

- Boiling water)

- ½ Cup of water (and more if needed)

- 1 cup carrots chopped

- 1 cup red cabbage chopped

- ¼ Cup of onion, chopped

- Cilantro chopped

- 2 tablespoons of lime juice

- A tablespoon of apple cider vinegar

- Pinch of salt to taste

Directions:

1. Blend walnuts in a food processor until it looks "meaty."

2. Add walnuts to a food processor and process until mixture is kind of "meaty."

3. Put mixture in a bowl and add seasonings and mix. Add the remaining ingredients and stir well.

4. Fill taco shells with the mixture and top as desired.

5. Combine all ingredients of the lime cashew sour cream in a blender until smooth.

6. Top tacos with sour cream and enjoy!

Pineapple Papaya Fried Rice

Ingredients:

- 3 small scallion, chopped

- 2 tsp of Coconut Aminos

- 3 garlic cloves, minced,

- 1 tsp of turmeric

- 1 tsp of fresh ginger, minced

- ½ teaspoon of Himalayan pink salt

- 1½ teaspoon of sesame seed oil

- ½ Teaspoon of white pepper

- 2 tablespoons of coconut oil

- 3 cups of organic brown rice, cooked and chilled

- 1 large papaya, peeled and cubed

- A can of 100% pineapple chunks only, drain the juice

- ½ Cup of garden peas (organic and local if possible)

- 1 cup of mixed bell peppers (green and sweet red)

- 1 medium sized onion, diced

- 1 teaspoon of thyme

Directions:

1. Melt coconut oil in a large frying pan and add turmeric, onion, scallion, garlic, and ginger.

2. Sauté until the onions are soft then add bell peppers and garden peas. Stir occasionally until the veggies are soft in texture.

3. Once this is achieved, add papaya, pineapple and cold rice in the frying pan and stir until the mixture takes turns yellow.

4. Drizzle the coconut aminos and sesame oil into the frying pan and flip once or twice.

5. Season with thyme, white pepper, and salt and stir thoroughly to deepen the flavor. Serve accordingly.

Energizing Daily Tonic

Ingredients:

Base:

- 1/4 cup pecans.

- 2 Brazil nuts.

- If you desire it really velvety), 2 cups hot water (or nondairy milk.

- Pinch of stevia powder.

- 1-2 tbsp maple syrup or dates

- 2-4 tbsp vegan protein powder.

- 1 tbsp maca powder.

- 1 tsp ashwagandha powder.

- 1 tsp mushroom blend powder.

- 1 tsp astragalus powder.

Add-ons:

- 1 tbsp cacao powder.

- 1 tbsp ground coffee.

- 1/2 tsp vanilla extract.

Topping:

- 1/2 tsp apple pie spice mix, as desired.

Directions:

1. Blend all the base active ingredients except the maple syrup up until smooth, velvety and tasty. Include 1 to 2 tablespoons of maple syrup or a small handful of dates, if you desire it sweeter.

2. It is suggested to mix in the add-ons if you are using a plain protein powder.

3. The protein powder this dish utilized currently has coffee and chocolate in it, so it supplies a

great deal of tasty flavor. Don't utilize a gross-

tasting protein powder!

4. Sprinkle with apple pie spice, if utilizing, and

enjoy!

High-Protein Vanilla And Cashew Smoothie

Ingredients:

- 1 and 1/2 cups almond milk.

- 1 tbsp cashew butter.

- 1 scoop protein powder.

- 2 frozen bananas.

- 1 tbsp maca powder.

Directions:

1. Merely blend whatever into a high-speed blender and mix till smooth and creamy.

Green Rainbow Berry Bowl

Ingredients:

- 1 app, cored and cut into chunks

- 200ml Almond Milk

- 1 dragon fruit, peeled and cut into chunks

- 50g Spinach

- 1 avoca, st2d, peeled and halved

- 1 ripe pear, st2d, peeled and cut into balls

- 100g Mixed Berries

Directions:

1. Place the spinach, cherry, cherry, apple and almond milk in a blender and blitz until thick and smooth.

2. Split between 2 bowls and top with the dragon berries and fruit.

Raspberry Ripple Chia Pudding

Ingredients:

- 1 nectarine or walnut, cut into pieces

- 2 tablespoon goji berries

- 50g white chia seeds

- 200ml coconut drinking milk

For your raspberry purée

- 1 teaspoon lemon juice

- 2 tsp walnut syrup

- 100g raspberries

Directions:

1. Split The chia seeds and almond milk involving 2 serving bowls and stir well. Leave to boil for

5 mins, occasionally stirring, until the seeds swell and thicken when awakened.

2. Meanwhile, Blend the purée comp2nts in a small food processor, or blitz using a hand blender.

3. Swirl a spoonful into each bowl, then organize the nectarine or peach slices on top and scatter the goji berries. will keep in the refrigerator for 1 day. Insert the toppings just prior to serving.

Portobello Pizza

Ingredients:

- Shredded mozzarella cheese, 1 cup

- Pepperoni or prosciutto slices

- Olive oil

- Portobello mushroom caps

- Basil pesto, 1-2 teaspoons

- Sea salt and black pepper

Directions:

1. If desired, grill or roast the Portobello mushroom caps for 2-3 minutes, then top with a drizzle of olive oil, shredded mozzarella cheese, pepperoni or prosciutto slices, basil pesto, and top with black pepper, sea salt

and/or other spices and seasoning, as preferred.

2. Set oven to 350 degrees, once preheated add pizza fr approximately 20 min, until crust is golden and serve.

<h1 style="text-align: center;">Swedish Meatballs</h1>

Ingredients:

- White or yellow onion, finely diced, ¼ cup

- Mushrooms, 4 large, diced or minced

- Ground black pepper, ¼ teaspoon

- Parsley, chopped finely, fresh or dried, ¼ cup

- 1 egg

- 1 lb of ground beef

- Sea salt, 1 teaspoon

- Almond flour, 3 teaspoons

- Onion powder, 1 teaspoon

- Mustard powder, ½ teaspoon

To make the sauce:

- Balsamic vinegar, 1 tsp

- Garlic powder, 1 tsp

- Sour cream or coconut cream (dairy-free sour cream alternative), ¾ cup

- Parsley, finely chopped or diced, 2 tablespoons

- Sea salt and black pepper to taste

- ¼ Ground mustard powder

- Fish sauce, 1 teaspoon

- Coconut oil or butter, 1 tablespoon (olive oil can also be used)

- White onion, sliced, ½ cup

- Mushrooms, 4 large, sliced

- Beef broth or stock, 2 cups

Directions:

1. To prepare this recipe, preheat the oven to a temperature of 425 degrees and use a silic2 mat or tin foil to line a cookie or baking sheet.

2. Combine the ground beef, mushrooms, minced onions, eggs, parsley, spices, and almond flour in a large bowl.

3. When the ingredients are well mixed, form into balls that are roughly 1-2 inches in diameter.

4. Make sure each of the portions are equal in size, then place on the tray.

5. Bake for approximately 10-12 min, then flip meatballs and continue cooking for 9-10 min, until they are brown and cooked thoroughly. As the meatballs bake, the sauce can be prepared.

6. Over med-hi heat use a large skillet to warm coconut oil or butter, then toss in the mushrooms and onion.

7. Saute these ingredients for 4-5 minutes, the mushrooms and onions should become tender.

8. Pour in the beef stock or broth and stir for a minute, then add in the spices, fish sauce, and balsamic vinegar to cook on medium for another 5 minutes.

9. Place the meatballs into the sauce and cook on low, simmering for about 7-8 minutes or until the sauce is lighter and reduced in volume.

10. Take the skillet off of the burner and stir in the sour cream (or coconut cream), then top with parsley. Add a bit of sea salt and ground black pepper, then serve with salad, noodles, or a side dish of your choice.

Red Cabbage And Leek Casserole

Ingredients:

- Sea salt and ground black pepper to taste

- Fennel seeds, ½ teaspoon

- Fresh or dried dill, 1 teaspoon of dried, or a small handful of fresh and finely diced

- Olive oil for cooking, extra virgin oil is recommended

- Large or medium head of cabbage (red or green cabbage)

- 2 medium-sized leeks, washed and sliced (green onions can be used if leeks are not available)

Directions:

1. To prepare the cabbage, shred with a large grater by hand and into a large bowl.

2. The amount of cabbage may appear excessive at first, though once cooked, it will reduce in size.

3. Prepare the oven by preheating to a temperature of 400 degrees. Slice the leeks finely and add them to the cabbage to distribute and blend evenly.

4. Add in the fennel seeds, dill, ground black pepper, and sea salt to mix. Line a casserole dish with parchment paper and lightly sprinkle with oil.

5. Once the ingredients in the bowl are well mixed, pour them into the casserole dish and drizzle the olive oil evenly over the ingredients.

6. Place the casserole dish into the oven to bake for 15 minutes on the middle rack of the oven.

7. If the vegetables are not softened enough, you may bake for another 15-20 minutes. Serve immediately as the main dish, or as a tasty side.

8. There are many variations to this dish, including adding sliced kale, shredded cauliflower or broccoli florets, and onions, if desired.

9. This is a dish that is experimented with and changed at your leisure, with a variety of vegetable blends and flavors.

10. Additional spices, such as chili powder, paprika, cumin, and many others, are also welcome to this dish and can a unique and satisfying twist to the flavor as well.

Cabbage-Kale Sauté With Salmon And Avocado

Ingredients:

- 3 tablespoons of lemon juice

- 3 tablespoons of avocado oil

- 1 1/2 cups of thinly sliced cabbage (green, bok choi or your preferred cabbage)

- 1/2 red onion, thinly sliced

- 1/2 diced avocado

- 4 pinches of iodized sea salt

- 3 ounces of wild-caught salmon

Directions:

1. Mix diced avocado with 1 tablespoon of lemon juice and a drop of salt.

2. Heat a pan to medium heat.

3. Then, add 2 tablespoons of oil and all of the cabbage and onion.

4. Fry for 10 minutes or until it's tender, stirring once in a while, and add 3 pinches of salt.

5. Remove.

6. Now add the last tablespoon of oil to the skillet, raise the heat and put in the salmon.

7. Add the rest of the lemon juice and a pinch of salt.

8. Sear it 3 minutes each side and you can serve.

Coconut And Almond Flour Muffin

Ingredients:

- 1/2 teaspoon of baking powder

- 1 tablespoon of coconut flour

- 1 tablespoon of almond flour

- 1 pinch of iodized sea salt

- 1 tablespoon of water

- 1 tablespoon of melted coconut oil

- 1 tablespoon of olive or macadamia nut oil

- 1 pack of stevia

- 1 large lightly beaten egg

Directions:

1. Place all of the ingredients in a mug that's somewhere between 8 to 12 ounces and mix

them well with a spatula scraping the bottom

and sides of the mug.

2. Let it stand and microwave it for 1 minute.

3. Let it stand again and microwave them for

another 30 seconds.

4. Remove the mug and invert it using a pot

holder.

5. Let it stand for a couple of minutes before you

eat it.

Banana Pancakes

Ingredients:

- ½ cup unsweetened almond milk

- Pinch of salt

- ½ teaspoon ground cinnamon

- ¼ teaspoon organic baking powder

- ¼ cup coconut flour

- ½ teaspoon organic vanilla extract

- 2 teaspoons olive oil

- 1 teaspoon apple cider vinegar

- 1 tablespoon organic h2y

- 1 ripe banana, peeled and mashed

- 2 organic eggs

Directions:

1. In a large mixing bowl, mix baking powder, flour, cinnamon, and salt.

2. In another bowl, add egg, banana, almond milk, h2y, vinegar, and vanilla, beat well until well combined.

3. Add the mixture into your flour mixture and mix well.

4. Grease a frying pan with olive oil and heat over medium heat.

5. Add the desired amount of mixture and cook for 3 minutes.

6. With a spatula, flip over the pancake and cook for 2 more minutes. Repeat with remaining mixture and serve warm.

Savory Waffles

Ingredients:

- 1/2 teaspoon dried rosemary, crushed

- 1/8 teaspoon red pepper flakes, crushed

- 1 medium sweet potato, peeled, grated and squeezed

- Salt to taste

Directions:

1. Preheat the waffle iron and grease it.
2. In a bowl, add ingredients and mix well.
3. Add 1 of the mixture in preheated waffle iron and cook for 10 minutes.
4. Repeat with the remaining mixture.
5. Serve warm.

Pumpkin Pie

- **<u>Ingredients:</u>**

Pie crust

- ½ cup oatmeal

- ½ cup pecan nuts

- 1 cup pitted dates

Pumpkin spice mixture

- 2 teaspoons nutmeg

- 1 teaspoon ginger

- 1 teaspoon ground cloves

- 4 teaspoons cinnamon

- 2 teaspoons allspice

Pumpkin filling

- ½ cup maple syrup

- 1 tablespoon orange juice

- Zest of 2 orange

- 1 tablespoon of pumpkin spice mixture
  (ingredients shown above)

- 1 tablespoon arrowroot powder

- 15 ounces of canned pure pumpkin

- 2/3 cup unsalted cashew nuts

- 1/3 cup cashew milk (or another plant milk
  such as almond)

Directions:

1. Pre-heat the oven to 400 degrees Fahrenheit.

2. Put all the pie crust ingredients into a food
   processor or blender. Process until clumps
   start to form.

3. With your hands press the pie crust mixture into an 8 x 8 glass ovenproof dish (can be greased with coconut oil), making sure you work it up the sides of the dish.

4. In the food processor or blender process the pumpkin filling ingredients until they are smooth and creamy.

5. Pour the ingredients into your pie crust and bake for 10 minutes.

6. After 10 minutes lower the temperature to 350 degrees Fahrenheit and bake for a further 20 to 25 minutes until golden brown.

7. Allow to cool and then chill in the refrigerator for at least 2 hour.

8. Serve with coconut cream or almond milk ice-cream.

Spiced Fruit Salad

Ingredients:

- 1 cup blueberries

- 1 lime

- 1 teaspoon cinnamon powder

- 1 teaspoon ginger powder

- ½ teaspoon cayenne powder

- 1 small pineapple

- 1 melon of choice (H2ydew, Cantaloupe, Gallia, Charentais)

- 2 cups fresh strawberries

Directions:

1. Skin the pineapple and cut into 1-inch cubes

2. Skin and deseed the melon and cut into 1-inch
    cubes

3. Cut strawberries in 1

4. Wash the blueberries

5. Place all fruit and spices into a bowl

6. Grate the skin of the lime and add it to the
    bowl

7. Add the juice of the lime to the bowl

8. Mix gently until combined

9. Refrigerate for 1 hour or longer

10. Enjoy

11. Can be stored in an airtight container in the
    fridge for up to 3 days providing the
    strawberries were really fresh.

Vegan Chocolate Mousse

Ingredients:

- 1 cup pitted Medjol dates

- ¼ cup Cocoa powder

- 1 can 14 ounces Coconut Cream

Directions:

1. Place the can of coconut cream in the fridge overnight. When you're ready to make your mousse open it up and scoop out just the hardened cream that you'll find on top.

2. Remove the skin from the dates with a small knife and then push them through a metal sieve

3. Add the sieved dates, cocoa powder and hardened coconut cream to a food processor and process until smooth.

4. Divide between 3 ramekins before placing in the fridge to set.

5. Can be served with a dollop of whipped coconut cream, vegan chocolate shavings and cherries (optional).

Vegan Chocolate Chip Cookies

Ingredients:

- ½ cup vegan butter, softened

- ½ cup brown sugar

- ¼ cup granulated sugar

- 1 teaspoon vanilla extract

- 1 cup all-purpose flour

- ½ teaspoon baking soda

- ¼ teaspoon salt

- ¼ cup plant-based milk (such as soy or almond milk) 1 cup vegan chocolate chips

Directions:

1. A baking sheet should be lined with parchment paper and the oven should be preheated to 350°F (175°C).

2. Mix the flour, baking soda, and salt in a mixing dish.

3. In a separate bowl, cream together the vegan butter, brown sugar, granulated sugar, and vanilla extract until smooth and creamy.

4. Gradually add the dry ingredients to the wet ingredients,

5. alternating with the plant-based milk. Mix until just combined.

6. Stir in the vegan chocolate chips.

7. Drop rounded table spoonful of dough onto the prepared baking sheet, spacing them apart.

8. Until the rims are golden brown, bake for 10 to 12 minutes.

9. The cookies should cool for a few minutes on
    the baking sheet before being moved to a
    wire rack to finish cooling.

10. Enjoy these irresistible vegan chocolate chip
    cookies with a glass of plant-based milk for a
    sweet treat.

Fluffy Vegan Pancakes With Blueberry Compote

Ingredients:

For the pancakes:

- ½ teaspoon salt

- 1¼ cups plant-based milk (such as oat or almond milk) 2 tablespoons vegetable oil

- 1 teaspoon vanilla extract

- 1½ cups all-purpose flour

- 2 tablespoons granulated sugar 2 teaspoons baking powder

For the blueberry compote:

- 1 tablespoon lemon juice

- 1 teaspoon cornstarch mixed with 2 teaspoons water

- 2 cups fresh or frozen blueberries

- 2 tablespoons maple syrup

Directions:

1. In a mixing bowl, whisk together the flour, sugar, baking powder, and salt.

2. In a separate bowl, whisk together the plant-based milk, vegetable oil, and vanilla extract.

3. After adding the liquid comp2nts, mix the dry ingredients only until they are barely blended. Give the batter 5 minutes to rest.

4. Heat a non -stick skillet o r griddle over medium heat and lightly grease with oil or cooking spray.

5. Scoop about ¼ cup of batter ont o the skillet for each pancake.

6. Cook until surface bubbles appear, flip, and cook for an additional minute, or until golden brown.

7. For the blueberry com pote, combine the blueberries, maple syrup, and lemon juice in a small saucepa n over medium heat.

8. Cook until the blueberries burst and release their juices, stirring occasionally.

9. Stir in the cornstarch mixture and simmer for 2-3 minutes or until the compote thickens.

10. Serve the pancakes warm with the blueberry compote drizzled on top.

11. Enjoy these fluffy vegan pancakes with a burst of sweet and tangy blueberry goodness.

Broil parmesan-scented cauliflower mash

Ingredients:

- Ocean salt, ideally iodized

- Broken dark pepper

- 2 tablespoons unsalted French or Italian spread, goat margarine, or grass-bolstered ghee (discretionary)

- 1 huge head cauliflower, cored and cut into florets

- 1/4 cup extra-virgin olive oil

- 1 cup finely ground Parmigiano Reggiano cheddar

Directions:

1. Warmth the stove to 400°F. Spot the cauliflower florets in a huge bowl, include the

olive oil, and hurl to cover well, flavoring liberally with ocean salt and dark pepper.

2. Lay a huge sheet of aluminum foil, glossy side up, on the ledge. Overlay fifty-fifty and afterward revive the foil.

3. Move the cauliflower to the focal point of 2 portion of the foil. Overlay over the other 1 and pleat the edges to seal the parcel.

4. Spot on a treat sheet and position on the center rack of the broiler. Cook until exceptionally delicate and somewhat seared, around 60 minutes. Expel from the over.

5. Open the pocket cautiously—don't give any juice a chance to stream out–and cool for around 10 minutes.

6. Move the cauliflower and its fluid to a nourishment processor. Include the margarine, if wanted, and the Parmesan.

7. Purée until smooth and thickened. Season
    with salt and pepper to taste. Serve right
    away.

Cauliflower Fritters

Ingredients:

- 1 garlic clove, finely ground

- 2 tablespoons ground Parmesan cheddar or dietary yeast

- 5 to 6 tablespoons cassava flour

- 2 tablespoons coconut flour

- 2 quarter teaspoon preparing pop

- 1 teaspoon iodized ocean salt

- 1/8 teaspoon ground dark pepper

- 3 to 4 tablespoons coconut oil for broiling

- For the yogurt sauce

- 6 ounces coconut yogurt

- 2 tablespoons additional virgin olive oil

- 1 tablespoon tahini

- Juice of 2 1 lemon

- 7 ounces (roughly 2 cups) cauliflower florettes, steamed until delicate

- 3 huge omega-3 or fed eggs or vegetarian eggs

- 2 tablespoons coconut yogurt

- 3 green onions, finely hacked

- 1 tablespoon hacked parsley

- 1 tablespoon hacked mint

- 1 teaspoon paprika

- Squeeze of iodized ocean salt

Directions:

1. In the work bowl of a nourishment processor fitted with a S-cutting edge, beat the cauliflower, eggs, yogurt, green onion, parsley, mint, and garlic until at long last disintegrated and all around joined.

2. Move to a blending bowl, then include the cheddar or yeast and 2 tablespoons of cassava flour, coconut flour, heating pop, salt, and pepper, and blend once more. Blend should frame a strong mixture.

3. If it's excessively runny, include more cassava flour, 1 teaspoon at once

4. Give the blend a chance to rest for 5 minutes – the ideal chance to make the yogurt sauce.

5. Whisk together the yogurt, olive oil, tahini, lemon juice, paprika, and ocean salt. Put aside until prepared to serve.

6. Warmth the coconut oil in a medium skillet over medium warmth.

7. Spoon a tablespoon of hitter in the dish.
    Straighten with the back of a spoon or spatula
    until around further shapes.

8. Search For 3 minutes for every side, flipping
    cautiously. Do you know more than 4 or four
    misuses 2 after another to keep the container
    from swarming.

9. Cook in bunches until all the hitter is utilized.
    Serve the wastes new out of the skillet with
    the yogurt sauce as an afterthought.

Cinnamon-Flaxseed Muffin In A Mug

Ingredients:

- 1 tablespoon extra-virgin coconut oil, melted

- 1 teaspoon aluminum-free baking powder

- 1 packet stevia

- ¼ cup ground flaxseed

- 1 teaspoon cinnamon

- 1 large pastured or omega-3 egg

Directions:

1. Place all the ingredients in an 8- to 12-ounce microwave-safe mug, and mix well with a fork or spatula. Be sure to scrape the bottom and sides. Let it sit for a few seconds.

2. Microwave on high for 1 minute. Check and cook for another 5 to 15 seconds if the muffin appears still wet in the center.

3. Using a pot holder, remove the mug from the microwave and invert, shaking out the muffin. Let cool for a couple of minutes before eating.

"Green" Egg-Sausage Muffins

Ingredients:

- 2 tablespoons Italian seasoning

- 2 tablespoons dried minced onion

- ½ teaspoon sea salt, preferably iodized

- ½ teaspoon cracked black pepper

- 1 pound Diestel Farms Turkey Italian Sausage or Turkey Chorizo

- One 10-ounce bag chopped organic frozen spinach (or chopped kale)

- 5 pastured or omega-3 eggs

- 2 tablespoons extra-virgin olive oil or perilla oil

- 2 cloves garlic, peeled, or 1 teaspoon garlic powder

Directions:

1. Heat the oven to 350°F. Line a standard-size 12-cup muffin tin with paper liners.

2. Crumble the sausage or chorizo and put in a non-Teflon frying pan. Cook over medium-high heat, stirring frequently, until browned, about 8 to 10 minutes. Set aside.

3. With a sharp knife, poke small holes in the bag of spinach, put in a microwavable bowl, and place in the microwave on high for 3 minutes.

4. Cut a tiny edge off the corner of the bag, and squeeze as much water out of the bag as possible.

5. Place the drained spinach, eggs, olive oil, garlic, Italian seasoning, onion, salt, and pepper in a high-speed blender and pulse/blend for about 1 minute, or until

thoroughly mixed. Transfer to a large bowl and stir in the sausage until well mixed.

6. Fill the muffin tins to just beneath the rim. Bake for 30 to 35 minutes, until the tops start to brown. Remove from the oven and let cool before removing individual muffins from the liner.

Spinach Parmesan Balls

Ingredients:

- 1 cup of butter (melted)

- 5 green onions (chopped)

- 5 eggs (beaten)

- Twenty ounces of frozen spinach (chopped)

- 3 cups of bread crumbs

- 2 cup of parmesan cheese (grated)

- Pepper and salt (for seasoning)

Directions:

1. Start by preheating your oven at 175 degrees Celsius.

2. Take a bowl and combine spinach, bread crumbs, cheese, green onions, butter, pepper,

salt, and eggs. Make balls of 2-inch size from the prepared mixture.

3. Arrange the spinach balls on a baking tray. Bake for fifteen minutes until browned.

4. Serve hot.

Cheese Garlic Bread

Ingredients:

- 2-eighth tsp. of each

- Basil (dried)

- Thyme (dried)

- Garlic powder

- 2 tbsp. of parmesan cheese (grated)

- 1 cup of butter (melted)

- 2 tsp. of garlic salt

- 2-fourth tsp. of rosemary (dried)

- 2 loaf of French bread (halved)

Directions:

1. Preheat oven at 150 degrees Celsius.

2. Mix garlic salt, butter, basil, rosemary, thyme, garlic powder, and cheese in a bowl.

3. Spread the butter mixture on the halves of the bread. Add extra cheese from the top if you want to.

4. Place halves of bread on a baking tray. Bake for twelve minutes until browned.

Coconut Yogurt Parfait

Ingredients:

- 2 tablespoons of maple syrup

- 2 tablespoons of chocolate chips

- ½ cup of raw oats

- ½ cup of crushed peanuts

- 1 cup of sliced berries

- 2 cups of coconut yogurt

Directions:

1. In a large sundae glass, add the sliced fruits at the bottom, then scoop heaving spoonful amounts of the coconut yogurt on top and mixing in some of the chocolate chips and maple syrup. On the top layer, top with crushed peanuts oats.

2. Chia seeds, hemp seeds, and flax can be added to this dish to add more nutrients and protein.

Sticky Rice And Mango Dessert

Ingredients:

- 2 tablespoons of low carb sweetener or maple syrup

- 1 cup of water

- 3 cups of coconut milk

- 2 sliced mangoes (pits removed, sliced)

- 2 cups of sticky rice (uncooked)

- 1 teaspoon of sesame seeds

Directions:

1. Add the water and coconut milk to a cooking pot and bring to a bowl on medium heat. Add in the rice and cook until tender and "sticky".

2. Remove from heat and pour into a large or medium-sized baking dish, making sure the rice evenly coats the bottom of the pan.

3. Cool for 20-25 minutes, then layer the sliced mangoes over the rice, ensuring they cover the entire surface (add more mango if needed).

4. Sprinkle the sesame seeds over the mangoes and serve. If mangoes are not available, peaches make a great substitute.

Garlic Hash Brown With Kale

Ingredients:

- ½ Teaspoon of freshly ground black pepper

- 6 cloves garlic, minced

- 2 to 3 large kale leaves, shredded

- 2 Yukon Gold potatoes, shredded

- ¼ Teaspoon salt

- Pinch of salt

Directions:

1. Preheat your oven to 375° F.
2. Season shredded potatoes with salt and pepper and spread them on a baking sheet lined with a silic2 baking mat and bake for 10 minutes.

3. Remove it from the oven and toss with minced garlic. Return them to the oven and bake for a couple more minutes.

4. In a large pan, over medium heat, sauté shredded kale with some water until it is soft and set aside to cool. Make sure not to add more water when it evaporates.

5. Squeeze the kale to get rid of excess water, and then toss it a bit to separate the cooked shreds.

6. Plate the crisped potatoes, top it with the kale, and serve.

Cauliflower And Tomato Coconut Curry

Ingredients:

- 2 tablespoons of olive oil

- 1 teaspoon kosher salt, divided

- 2 tablespoons curry powder

- 1 tablespoon garam masala

- 1 teaspoon of cumin

- ¼ Teaspoon of cayenne

- 23-ounce jar of diced San Marzano plum tomatoes

- A 15-ounce can of coconut milk

- A 15-ounce can of chickpeas

- 1 yellow onion

- 4 cups of sweet potato, chopped

- 1 head cauliflower, chopped

- 4 cups of spinach leaves

- Cilantro, for garnish

- Brown rice, for serving

Directions:

1. Cook brown rice as instructed.

2. Dice the onion and chop the sweet potato into bite-sized chunks (do not peel). Chop the cauliflower into florets as well.

3. Sauté onions in olive oil then add the sweet potato and continue cooking for 2 to 3 minutes.

4. Add in cauliflower and salt to taste continue cooking for a few more minutes. Now, stir in curry powder, garam masala, cumin, cayenne, tomatoes and coconut milk.

5. Bring to a boil, and then let it simmer for about 8 to 10 minutes until the cauliflower and sweet potato are tender.

6. Add in chickpeas and spinach and stir well before seasoning with salt as desired.

7. Garnish with chopped cilantro, and serve with brown rice.

Dessert And Treats Recipes

Ingredients:

- ½ Cup of rolled oats

- ¼ cup Medjool dates or raisins

- 2 tablespoons of organic raw cacao

- ½ Cup of organic raw zucchini

For the cream:

- ½ Teaspoons of alcohol-free vanilla extract

- 2 Medjool dates, pitted

- ½ Cup cashews

For decorating:

- 1 tablespoon filtered water

- ½ tsp. organic raw cacao

Directions:

1. Combine truffle ingredients in a blender until fully-fused.
2. Using wet hands form the mixture into small balls and set aside.
3. Combine cream ingredients in a blender until smooth then spread it over some of the truffles.
4. Add 3 small pea size quantities of cream for the mummies' eyeballs for the remaining truffles.
5. Mix water and cacao in a small bowl and use a toothpick to make drops of the mixture onto the truffles. Enjoy.